A *fashionable* HISTORY *of* JEWELLERY & ACCESSORIES

A FASHIONABLE HISTORY OF JEWELLERY &
ACCESSORIES
was produced by

David West 🯅🯅 Children's Books

7 Princeton Court
55 Felsham Road
London SW15 1AZ

Author: Helen Reynolds
Editor: Jackie Gaff
Picture Research: Carlotta Cooper
Designer: Julie Joubinaux

First published in Great Britain in 2003 by
Heinemann Library, Halley Court, Jordan Hill,
Oxford OX2 8EJ, a division of
Harcourt Education Ltd.

OXFORD MELBOURNE AUCKLAND
JOHANNESBURG BLANTYRE GABORONE
IBADAN PORTSMOUTH (NH) USA CHICAGO

07 06 05 04 03
10 9 8 7 6 5 4 3 2 1

ISBN 0 431 18331 7 (HB)
ISBN 0 431 18339 2 (PB)

British Library Cataloguing in Publication Data

Reynolds, Helen
A fashionable history of jewellery and accessories
1. Jewelry - History - Juvenile literature 2. Dress
accessories - History - Juvenile literature
3. Fashion - History - Juvenile literature
I. Title II. Jewellery and accessories
391.4'4'09

Printed and bound in China

*An explanation of difficult words can be
found in the glossary on page 31.*

A *fashionable* HISTORY *of* JEWELLERY & ACCESSORIES

Heinemann
LIBRARY

Contents

THE RIGHT TOOL FOR THE JOB

Jewellers were using this kind of strap drill to pierce beads by about 6,000 years ago. As tools and techniques improved, so did the quality of the finished jewellery.

ANCIENT AMULET

Crafted here into a contemporary ring, the Eye of Horus was one of the most powerful ancient Egyptian amulets.

PASSING THE TIME OF DAY

The wristwatch became a fashion accessory in the late 19th century. Before this time, watches were mainly hung from a chain or tucked into a pocket.

From beads to mobiles

ACCESSORIES DATE BACK TO PREHISTORIC TIMES, when our ancestors began decorating themselves with beads and other ornaments, and sewing animal skins into mittenlike bags to keep their hands warm. Most accessories have been created for either practical or vain reasons, although superstition has also played an important role and, for centuries, charms called amulets were believed to protect the wearer from bad luck or illness. Fashions in accessories have come and gone over the years, but the greatest change has taken place in the past few decades. Whereas in the past, few people felt dressed without jewellery or gloves, today's essential finishing touch is electronic – the mobile phone.

UP TO DATE

In the 1980s, the Filofax diary became high fashion and an essential accessory.

A WORLD OF ORNAMENT

In some parts of the world, jewellery has been used to stretch and shape body parts such as the neck, as well as to decorate them.

PRACTICE MAKES PERFECT

Brooches began life as functional objects, used in ancient times to pin clothes together.

ELECTRONIC FASHION ACCESSORY

The first mobile phones were black and the size of a brick. Today's models are small enough to fit inside a pocket and come in all colours of the rainbow to match any outfit, night or day.

FROM BRIEFCASE TO BACKPACK

The backpack came into fashion in the 1980s. It is a useful alternative to the briefcase and the handbag.

Adorning the neck

NECKLACES WERE PROBABLY THE FIRST JEWELLERY to be worn. More than 30,000 years ago, our prehistoric ancestors began piercing holes in plant seeds, seashells and animal teeth, and threading them on strings made from plant fibres or strips of animal hide. Animal bones, antlers and ivory were also shaped into beads or amulets – charms believed to bring luck and keep away evil spirits.

All that glitters

In many cultures around the world, gold has long been valued above all other materials. This Sumerian gold jewellery was made more than 4,500 years ago.

Setting the gold standard

As the centuries passed and the first civilizations grew up in the Middle East, jewellery-making techniques became more sophisticated and materials such as gold came to be highly valued. Some of the earliest-known pieces of gold jewellery were crafted more than 4,500 years ago. They were found in the graves of the kings and queens of Sumeria, a civilization that flourished in the region we now call southeastern Iraq.

Material differences

In some parts of the world different materials were rated more highly than gold. Copper and turquoise were prized by the Native North American Indians (above).

Around the world in many ways

Necklace shapes and styles have also varied worldwide and throughout history. Beaded collars are traditional in many parts of Africa, for example.

Variations on a theme

Throughout history jewellery styles and materials have varied from culture to culture, and from one fashion era to another. In Europe in the 15th century, for instance, wearing a pendant on an extremely long chain became stylish. Religious pendants such as the crucifix were particularly popular. In the late 19th century, the throat-hugging choker was popularized by Queen Alexandra (1844–1925), who originally began wearing the style to cover a scar on her neck.

DEEP THROAT

Necklaces have not only been used to decorate the throat, as seen here on the singer Cher (b.1946), but also for body shaping (right). Rings are added gradually to stretch the neck.

CHAINED UP

Mr T, from the 1980s T.V. series, The A-Team, wore chunky chains – an exaggerated take on the fashion of the time.

GETTING COLLARED

Punks gave the 19th-century passion for the choker necklace a new twist in the 1970s, when they took to wearing real dog collars.

Bracelets & bangles

BRACELETS HAVE ALSO BEEN AROUND SINCE PREHISTORIC TIMES. *The earliest style was a simple string of beads, but by 4,000 years ago the ancient Egyptians were making bracelets with clasps. The Egyptians loved jewellery, and it was worn by men as well as women. In ancient Greece and Rome, however, bracelets and other jewellery were mainly womenswear. One of the most popular styles was a golden snake that twisted around the wrist and up the arm.*

Laying down the law

In Europe by the 13th century, bracelets had become unfashionable and were rarely worn, partly because the entire arm was usually covered by a full-length sleeve. Laws also began to be passed at this time, forbidding ordinary people from wearing precious metals and gemstones. It wasn't until sleeves grew shorter in the 18th century that it became stylish for wealthy women to wear bracelets once again. Sets of jewellery called parures became popular, and included matching earrings, rings, necklace and hair ornaments, as well as bracelets.

Ancient Egyptian arms

Ancient Egyptian women and men usually wore pairs of bracelets on both arms, often with a matching piece on the upper arm. Jewellery was also worn around the ankles.

Ethnic influences

Mass-produced modern jewellery such as this animal-skin bangle is often loosely based on traditional African designs.

Flaunting it

This woman from Rajasthan in India has used her cash to buy bangles. They are a sign of her wealth and she wears them all the time. It's also a good way of keeping an eye on them!

Stripping off for action

In the late 19th century, as women began to gain the vote and other freedoms, it became acceptable to bare the entire arm in a sleeveless dress. This further encouraged the wearing of bracelets. In the 1920s sunbathing became stylish for the first time, and burnished limbs were shown off by armfuls of bangles. Heavy, African-style designs in wood and ivory were particularly popular, but synthetic materials such as Bakelite (patented in 1909) were also introduced. The 20th century also saw a new take on the ancient amulet – the silver or gold charm bracelet laden with dozens of tiny, jingling trinkets.

IDENTITY PARADE

Identity bracelets were popular menswear by the 1960s. Made of silver or gold links, the bracelet carries a tag with the owner's name engraved into it.

SAYING IT WITH FLOWERS

Fresh flower corsages were traditionally presented to ladies by their partners and worn on the shoulders of their ball gowns. Here American students wear flowers at a school prom in 1997.

PLACING WATCHES ON SHOW

Wristwatches date from the late 19th century, when women began wearing them as jewellery. By 20 years later men had realized that a watch on your wrist was more practical than one in your pocket. These days wristwatches can be functional or highly ornamental. The watch above (left) has changeable faces to match a woman's different outfits.

Crowning glory

SINCE ANCIENT TIMES, CROWN-LIKE HEADDRESSES *have been worn by rulers as a symbol of their authority and power. The picture on the right shows one of the earliest-known royal headdresses. It was found in the grave of a Sumerian queen called Pu-abi, who died more than 4,500 years ago.*

Winning ways

Royal crowns were not always made of precious materials such as gold. The pharaohs of ancient Egypt wore a variety of crowns, the most important of which were the white and the red ceremonial crowns. Historians believe that these were made of cloth stretched over a frame. The pharaoh's everyday crown, the nemes, was made of striped cloth, but sometimes a gold circlet was worn instead.

Crowns were also sometimes awarded to non-royals, as a mark of excellence. In ancient Greece, for example, the prize for winning athletes at the Olympic Games was to be crowned with a wreath of olive leaves.

The Romans awarded a range of different crowns as military honours for prowess in battle. Some were wreaths made of laurel, olive or myrtle leaves, or flowers. Others were crafted from gold.

THE WINNER'S LAURELS

When Napoleon (1769–1821) crowned himself emperor of France in 1804, he based his crown on the wreaths awarded in Roman times.

SUMERIAN SPLENDOUR

Queen Pu-abi of Sumeria's headdress was made from gold flower and leaf shapes decorated with blue lapis lazuli and red cornelian.

EGYPTIAN EXCELLENCE

The solid gold mask found on the mummy of the boy pharaoh Tutankhamun (c.1344–27 BCE) showed him wearing the everyday nemes crown. The real nemes was made of cloth, not gold.

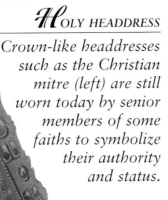

HOLY HEADDRESS

Crown-like headdresses such as the Christian mitre (left) are still worn today by senior members of some faiths to symbolize their authority and status.

QUEENING IT UP

When beauty pageants became popular during the 20th century, the beauty queens were often crowned with a glittering tiara – usually made from fake diamonds, not the real thing.

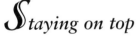

Staying on top

In Europe in the centuries that followed, elaborate, jewel-studded, gold or silver crowns came to be worn only by monarchs. From time to time, however, it was fashionable for people to wear circlets and other head ornaments as a sign of their status or wealth. Jewelled head ornaments became extremely popular for women in the 19th century, for instance. The most spectacular and expensive was the diamond tiara, which was worn only on special occasions such as a ball or a wedding.

THE GENUINE ARTICLE

The St Edward's Crown is only worn at the coronation of a new British monarch. The gold in it is thought to date from the 11th century.

Earrings & studs

ALTHOUGH EARRINGS WERE WORN BY SUMERIAN WOMEN AND MEN 4,500 years ago (see picture page 10), it was another 1,000 years before they appeared in Egypt. Egyptian earrings were mainly hoop- or disc-shaped, but studs were also sometimes worn. In ancient Greece and Rome, women were particularly fond of pendant styles.

ROMAN REMAINS

In ancient times, earrings were only for pierced ears. This Roman pair dates from the 3rd century CE.

Hanging loose

Like bracelets, earrings were rare in Europe by the late Middle Ages. They did not become stylish again until the late 16th century, when they were worn by both men and women. Pearl or jewelled pendants were favourite designs. Sometimes these were tied on the ear with a ribbon, instead of being hooked through a pierced lobe. Designs became more elaborate with the passing years, and in the 17th century flowers and bows were particularly popular. By the late 18th century, however, earrings were rarely seen on men.

PLUGGING THE GAP

In some parts of the world, it is traditional to decorate parts of the face permanently by inserting large plugs to stretch the skin.

(see picture page 10)

EYE, EYE, EYE

When Captain Kidd (below, c.1645–1701) terrorized the Caribbean, pirates and sailors wore earrings because it was believed that piercing the ears with precious metals such as gold improved the eyesight.

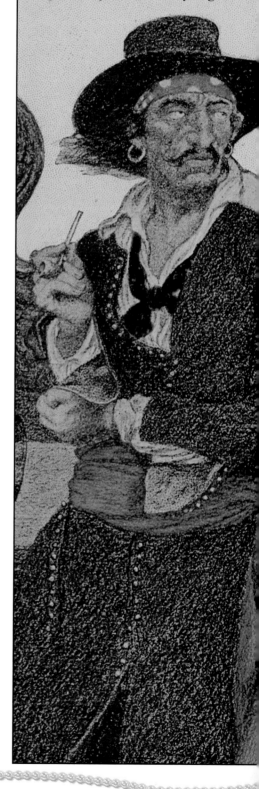

Faking it

In the mid-19th century, costume jewellery made from inexpensive or artificial materials began to be mass-produced, making it available to a wider range of women. Clip and screw fastenings were introduced, providing alternatives to piercing the earlobe. Novelty designs such as watering cans and wheelbarrows were also launched.

Costume jewellery really took off in the 1930s, however, after it was promoted by the fashion designers Coco Chanel (1883–1971) and Elsa Schiaparelli (1890–1973). Large, clip-on earrings became stylish, remaining so until the 1970s, when a craze for huge hooped earrings revived the popularity of designs for pierced ears.

Multiple choices

Although today a common sight on city streets the world over, multiple ear- and face-piercing was seen as a deeply shocking act of anti-establishment behaviour when it was taken up by punks in the late 1970s.

Modern manners

Their adoption by celebrities such as footballer David Beckham (b.1975) has helped relaunch earrings for men.

Lights on

It may seem like a novelty, but light-up jewellery dates back to the 1930s, when it was commissioned by Elsa Schiaparelli.

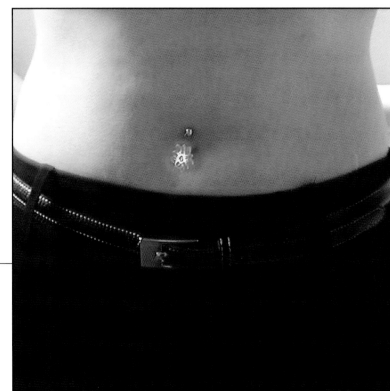

Rings on their fingers

STYLES HAVE CHANGED OVER THE CENTURIES, but rings have been worn since at least Sumerian times, when Queen Pu-abi was buried with one on each finger. Rings have also served different purposes, from the decorative to the functional. In ancient Egypt, for example, they were often engraved with the hieroglyphic symbols of the owner's name and used to stamp seals that fastened scrolls and other documents.

Sacred scarab

In ancient Egypt, the scarab beetle was the most common amulet, or good luck charm, and scarabs were often set into rings.

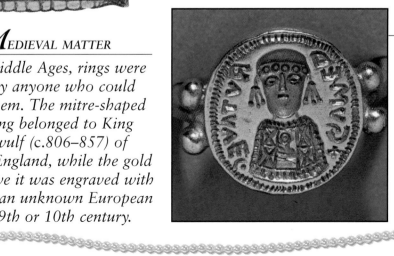

Keeping an eye on history

Contemporary designers often draw inspiration from the past. The shape of the ring above is based on the Eye of Horus, one of the most powerful ancient Egyptian good luck symbols.

Setting a standard

Seals were among the earliest objects to be set into rings, but by ancient Greek and Roman times, pearls and precious stones were also being used.

In the Middle Ages, the most highly prized gemstones were emeralds, sapphires and rubies. Diamonds were more difficult to cut and polish, and they didn't become popular in Europe until the 14th century, when sophisticated gem-cutting techniques were imported from Persia and India. Gemstones were still believed to have magical properties at this time – emeralds were thought to be an antidote to poison, for instance.

Medieval matter

In the Middle Ages, rings were worn by anyone who could afford them. The mitre-shaped gold ring belonged to King Ethelwulf (c.806–857) of Wessex, England, while the gold band above it was engraved with runes for an unknown European in the 9th or 10th century.

Seal of approval

This seal ring was inscribed with the name and portrait of its owner, Gumed-ruta, in the 6th or early 7th century, and is the earliest-known woman's seal ring. In later periods, rings were engraved with the family crest.

Romancing the stone

Over the centuries, advances in gem-cutting and setting techniques continued to improve the appearance of precious stones. In 1886, for example, the great American jewellers Tiffany & Co. devised a clawlike setting which held a single diamond high above the ring band. The Tiffany setting let far more light into the gem, making it sparkle even more brilliantly. It is still the most popular setting for diamonds today.

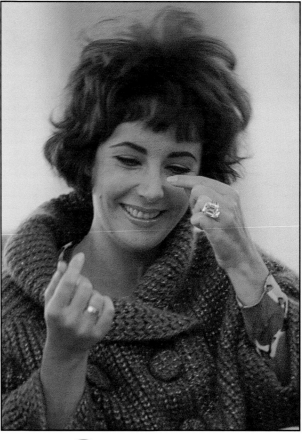

Fancy fingerwork

Throughout history, rings have been worn by men as well as women. It has often been fashionable to wear two or more rings on each finger, and sometimes to have rings on all the fingers and even the thumbs.

Diamonds are forever

One of the world's most famous diamonds, the 33.19-carat Krupp, was set into a ring and given to British-born actress Elizabeth Taylor (b.1932) by Richard Burton in 1968.

Banded for life

Wedding rings are thought to have first been given by the Romans. In the past they were often decorated – a linked-hands symbol was popular in Roman times.

Perfect pins

DECORATIVE BROOCHES DEVELOPED FROM THE PINS *used in ancient times to hold clothing together. The earliest looked like large versions of a dressmaker's pin. These then evolved into a cross between a safety pin and a brooch, called the fibula, the earliest of which were found in Italy.*

FABULOUS FIBULAE

This Etruscan fibula dates from 525–500 BCE. It is decorated with a popular mythological beast, the chimaera, which was composed of parts of various animals, in this case a lion and a goat.

Crafty Celts keep their independence

In central and northwestern Europe, the jewellery designs of the Celts developed independently from those of the Romans and other Mediterranean civilizations. Highly stylized animals and plants, and abstract patterns made up of elaborately interwoven curves and spirals were typical of Celtic art, and these designs were featured on everything from pottery to jewellery. The brooch was a key piece of Celtic jewellery, used as an ornamental fastening for cloaks and other garments.

FINE ARTISTRY

Jewellery designs have often echoed fine art styles. The swirling lines and stylized plant imagery of the brooches below are typical of the art nouveau movement of the late 19th century, for instance.

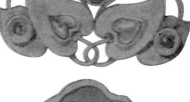

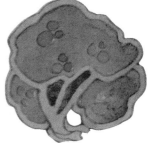

CELTIC CURVES

As seen in this present day re-enactment of an ancient Celtic battle, garments such as the plaid (right) were fastened with brooches. Interest in Celtic designs has been revived since the 19th century.

Colourful cameos

First created by the ancient Greeks more than 2,000 years ago, the cameo is a gemstone or shell with a raised design carved into it. The art of cameo carving had been lost by the Middle Ages, when ancient Greek and Roman cameos were popular brooch settings. It was rediscovered during the 17th century.

Badge of courage

Medals have been awarded for bravery in battle since ancient Egyptian times, when fly-shaped gold ornaments were given. In Europe, the first ribboned medals appeared in the 17th century.

Cheap & cheerful

Cheap metal badges have been decorating men and women's coat lapels since the 1840s, when a special cutting-and-stamping machine was invented. They have been used for everything from advertising slogans to political protest messages.

Perennial favourite

Unlike earrings and bracelets, brooches remained a key item of jewellery for men and women throughout the Middle Ages. They were less common in the 15th and 16th centuries, although noblemen sometimes decorated their hats with jewel-studded badges. Brooches regained popularity in the 17th century, however, and have been worn by women ever since.

As with other items of jewellery, brooch styles have kept pace with changing fashions. In the 18th century, for instance, court ladies decorated the front of their gowns with large brooches which covered the entire chest from neckline to waist. By the end of the 19th century, stylish women were wearing lots of small brooches, while in the early 20th century they often pinned a single, large brooch in the centre of a blouse collar.

Jewelled costumes

In some eras and parts of the world, nobles not only wore jewellery as free-standing pieces, but also had it sewn into their clothes. This might seem like a waste today, when fashions change so quickly, but in the past clothes were kept much longer and the fabric was often remodelled into a new garment.

Dressed to dazzle

Some of the most splendid jewelled costumes were worn by nobles at the Byzantine court – by the 6th century CE, the Byzantine Empire included parts of the Middle East, northern Africa, and southern and eastern Europe. Rich silks were woven with gold and silver threads, and oversewn with pearls and gemstones.

In western and northern Europe, jewellery and clothes were more restrained throughout the Middle Ages. By the early 16th century, however, stylish noblemen were wearing slashed doublets, or jackets, with the strips held together by jewel-encrusted clasps. The finest garments were worn by kings and queens as symbols of their wealth and power. Within decades, entire royal garments were being embroidered with hundreds of pearls, rubies, sapphires and diamonds.

DAPPER DRESSER

King Henry VIII (1491–1547) wore a slashed doublet dotted with square cut jewels. This was the height of male fashion in the 16th century.

ELEGANT EMPRESS

The borders of the sumptuous cloak and tunic worn by the Byzantine empress Theodora (c.500–548) were embroidered with gold thread and studded with precious stones.

Glittering prizes

During the next few centuries, it became fashionable for wealthy men and women to decorate their clothes with gold or jewelled buttons, and to have ornamental buckles on their shoes. Elaborate clothing gave way to simpler styles during the 19th century, particularly for daywear. But in the euphoric decade that followed World War I (1914–18), glamour took centre stage again and flappers danced the night away in low-waisted dresses decorated with sequins, beads and metallic thread.

Today, mass-produced synthetic materials have made glamour an affordable option for a broad range of people, not simply the rich. Depending on the latest trend, glittering outfits are once again worn any time, day or night.

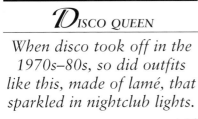

SHINING STAR

One of the most flamboyant male dressers of the 20th century was the American pianist and entertainer Liberace (1919–87). He was famous for his jewel-studded stage costumes and extravagant jewellery, as well as the candelabra that was always placed on his piano.

DISCO QUEEN

When disco took off in the 1970s–80s, so did outfits like this, made of lamé, that sparkled in nightclub lights.

The jeweller's art

THE STORY OF JEWELLERY *is not simply one of changing fashions, but also of the developing techniques of the jeweller. When prehistoric people began carving and piercing beads, they used a narrow stone blade called a burin. The drill had been invented by about 6,000 years ago.*

Timeless techniques

By Sumerian times, craftspeople had discovered how to refine gold and beat it into thin sheets. These were cut into flat shapes, such as the leaves on Queen Pu-abi's headdress (see page 10), or pressed over moulds to make 3-dimensional pieces. Various decorative techniques were developed in ancient times, including engraving (carving) and embossing or repoussé work (beating a metal sheet into a mould to make a raised design). Craftspeople also learned how to cast metals in moulds to make solid ornaments.

Hole in one

Strap drills like this were among the earliest to be invented. The drill bit was steadied in the mouth, then spun by pulling on a thong wrapped around it.

Steaming ahead

All jewellery was handmade until the 19th century, when the introduction of steam-powered machinery paved the way for mass production. The arrival of cheap, mass-produced jewellery did not spell the death of handcrafted pieces, however. The 20th century saw the rise of artist jewellers whose work, known as studio jewellery, is today sold in craft shops and exhibited in art galleries and museums the world over.

Magic & mystery

In ancient and medieval times, people known as alchemists attempted to find ways of changing ordinary metal into gold. Some were serious scientists, but many were fakes who tricked people with 'magical' spells and concoctions.

CUTTING, GRINDING & POLISHING

The craft of gem-cutting and polishing is called lapidary, and two main styles are practised. Stones cut in the cabochon style have a smooth, rounded top. For the faceted style, flat surfaces called facets are cut into the stone. Some of the main shapes invented over the centuries for faceted stones are shown below.

A gem can only be cut and polished by a material that is as hard as, or harder, than itself. After cutting, the stone is shaped with the bruting tool shown below. The bruting tool spins a harder gemstone at high speed to grind and smooth the softer one.

PANNING FOR GOLD

Panning is an ancient technique for extracting gold deposits from riverbeds. Gold is heavier than sand or mud, so it sinks to the bottom of a pan of water. Sand and mud are poured away in successive washings until the gold can be seen and removed.

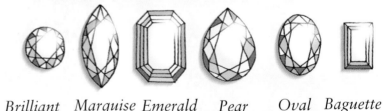

| Brilliant cut | Marquise cut | Emerald cut | Pear cut | Oval cut | Baguette cut |

SHINING LIGHTS

Few gemstones look beautiful in their raw state (inset picture). Cutting and polishing lets light into them, making them sparkle. When skilfully cut, a top-quality diamond glitters with all the colours of the rainbow.

SHARPEST SHAPE

The brilliant cut is today the most popular shape for diamonds. It has 58 facets and was invented towards the end of the 17th century, probably in Paris.

The handy bag

ALTHOUGH FEW WOMEN WOULD TODAY LEAVE HOME WITHOUT ONE, *the handbag is a relatively recent development in the history of fashion accessories. Bags have been used to carry things since prehistoric times, of course, but for centuries they were more functional than ornamental.*

Pockets, purses & reticules

Medieval clothes didn't have pockets, so men and women attached small purses or pouches to the beltlike girdle worn around their waist or hips. Wearing a purse outside your clothing was risky, and by the 14th century thieves were called cutpurses.

Although pockets were first sewn into men's clothes in the 16th century, both sexes continued to hang purselike bags around their waists. Women's skirts were huge in those days, and purses were easily hidden among the folds of fabric.

The first true handbag, the reticule, appeared in the 1790s when women began wearing high-waisted gowns that clung to the body, leaving no room to hide a bulky purse.

ARMED & READY FOR ACTION

First seen in the 1790s, reticules were made of velvet, satin or silk and decorated with embroidery and tassels. They were used to carry a purse, handkerchief and fan.

A beautiful evening bag was a must for the stylish 1920s woman. The most expensive were embroidered with beads, while the clasp was studded with gemstones. Inside, there was just enough room for a hankie and some make-up.

*H*andbags, briefcases & backpacks

Unlike reticules, which had drawstring tops, many of today's handbags are built around a sturdy frame and come with a clasp and one or two handles. This style of bag dates from the 1860s, when it was often made in leather.

The 20th century saw all sorts of handbag fashions for women, but most men continued to make do with pockets and briefcases. It wasn't until backpacks hit the high streets in the 1980s that men found a bag style to suit them.

*P*ICKING A GENTLEMAN'S POCKET

For centuries, after pockets were invented, thieves were known as pickpockets (left). The drawstring man's purse below was made in the 18th century.

*T*HE KELLY BAG

Princess Grace of Monaco (left, 1929–73, the former Hollywood actress Grace Kelly), made the classic Hermès handbag so famous that the company renamed it the Kelly bag in her honour in the 1950s.

*U*NISEX BAG

Traditionally used by hikers, the backpack was first adopted by men for general use in the early 1980s, and later by women as an alternative to the handbag.

Gloves, stoles & neckties

GLOVES WERE FIRST WORN IN PREHISTORIC TIMES, when people living in chilly northern Europe kept their fingers warm inside baglike coverings made from furry animal skins. In the warmer climate of Africa and the Mediterranean, gloves were first used to protect the hands. By Roman times, they were worn by workers and soldiers.

Mourning mittens

Black mittens and gloves were worn as a sign of mourning during the 19th century.

Handling a hawk

Medieval nobles loved to go hunting with hawks, and wore sturdy gauntlets to protect their hands from the birds' claws.

Taking up the gauntlet

Gloves came into widespread use during the Middle Ages, when most ordinary people wore mittens. Nobles preferred gauntlets – this style of glove had fingers and thumbs, fitted the hand closely, then broadened out at the wrist to cover much of the forearm.

By the 17th century, embroidered silk or leather gloves had become an essential part of a noble's costume. Glove shapes changed over the years, but until well into the 20th century it was customary for the upper classes to have gloves for day and evening wear. The well-dressed 19th-century gentleman, for example, usually wore coloured gloves in the day and white ones in the evening.

Dressed to go dancing

In the 19th century, ladies wore long gloves in the evening and a shorter pair in the day.

Dangerous driving

Although fashionable motoring wear in the early 20th century, long scarves could be dangerous. American dancer Isadora Duncan (1877–1927) was accidentally strangled when her scarf was caught in the wheels of her car.

Slipping on a stole

The stole or shawl dates back to ancient times, when a length of material was draped around the head and neck or wrapped around the shoulders. Scarves are shorter and narrower, and came along later. The term was first used in the 1590s, for a sash worn across the body by men. By the 1650s, men were tying small scarves called cravats around their necks, and in the 1840s they began wearing ties.

WRAPPINGS OF WEALTH

A long fur stole was a popular accessory for wealthy women by the early 20th century. Stoles had come back in vogue in the 1790s, when women began wearing dresses made from flimsy fabrics and needed the extra warmth.

SNUG AS A BUG

A tube-shaped muff was a stylish alternative to gloves from the late 16th century onwards, and was particularly fashionable for women in the 19th century.

FEATHERY FRIEND

Feather stoles called boas were fashionable in the 19th century, when they were often made from ostrich feathers.

Parasols, umbrellas & fans

PARASOLS OR SUNSHADES WERE INVENTED IN ANCIENT TIMES in the Middle and Far East, where they were often a symbol of royal or noble rank. Although the parasol was used by the ancient Greeks and Romans, it didn't become a fashion accessory in Europe until the 17th century.

Eastern import

Traders introduced the parasol to Europe from Japan and China in the late 16th century.

Form & function

The earliest European parasols, such as the one depicted above in a painting of the 1630s, were plain and functional. They became more decorative with the passing years.

Sunny disposition

The parasol was essential daywear for the fashionable lady until the early 20th century. The first designs were plain, but these were soon replaced by dainty items made of silk, satin or lace decorated with fringes or bows. When men began carrying waterproof umbrellas in the 18th century they were teased for being effeminate.

Pioneer on parade

English merchant and traveller Jonas Hanway (left, 1712–96) is said to have brought an umbrella back from Persia and been the first man to have walked the streets of London carrying one, in the 1750s.

Old favourite

A *flamboyantly large ostrich-feather fan was the height of fashion in the 1920s (left). Feather fans have been around for thousands of years, however, and were depicted in ancient Egyptian wall-paintings.*

History in hand

Fans were often handpainted. Made in the 1780s, this one commemorates the first successful hot-air balloon flights.

Fascinated by the fan

Although fans also date back to ancient times, the folding fan wasn't invented until about 1,700 years ago, in Japan. It became a firm favourite with European women after explorers brought it back from the East in the late 15th century, and it was still in common use in the 1920s. As well as its practical function as a cooling device, the fan also gave rise to a kind of flirtatious sign language – drawing it across the cheek meant 'I love you', for example.

National treasure

Introduced to Spain and Portugal from the East by explorers such as Marco Polo (1254–1324), the fan is still an essential part of both countries' national dress.

Sticking together

A walking stick made of lightweight cane or polished wood was sported by gentlemen from the late 16th to the late 19th century (above) and after.

Electronic accessories

A REVOLUTION IN FASHION ACCESSORIES WAS SPARKED IN 1971, when the marketing of the first microchip, the Intel 4004, announced the dawn of the modern electronic age. New technology has allowed us to carry our whole environment around with us, and electronic gadgets have become indispensable.

Small is beautiful

Mass production of the microchip led to a new generation of micro accessories. In the 1990s, computers went on a diet and slimmed from bulky boxes into slim rectangles, while mobile phones shrank from brick- to palm-size. Radios were whittled down to fit in the ear like a hearing aid, while watches were given everything from tiny TV screens to weather sensors.

Even clothes are now being given microchips. Aerials are woven into the fabric of these 'intelligent' outfits, and the collar is fitted with a tiny phone so the wearer can make calls or download information from the Internet.

ELECTRONIC ELEGANCE

Today's electronic personal organizers are small enough to fit in a handbag, and almost as elegant as a piece of jewellery.

28

CUSTOMIZING THE COMPUTER

When the first electronic computers were built in the 1940s, they were room-sized. Laptops were first marketed in the 1980s, and are now small enough to be carried and used anywhere.

ACCESSING THE INTERNET

The latest mobile phones provide Internet access, placing a whole world of information in the palms of our hands.

Coming out in colour

Early electronic accessories were expensive and rarely came in any colour other than black. Prices dropped as technological advances made production easier and faster, while styling improved as manufacturers competed to maintain their hold on the market. Shapes grew sleeker, and finishes became shinier and more colourful. Today's mobile phones come with interchangeable covers to match the wearer's outfit, for instance, while for the seriously wealthy, some companies offer models with solid gold cases encrusted with diamonds.

Walking out in style

Today also available as a CD player, the Walkman cassette player became one of the earliest electronic fashion accessories when it was launched by Sony in 1979.

*T*imeline

Prehistory
Jewellery was being worn 30,000 years ago. The earliest necklaces were made from seeds, seashells, feathers and animal bones and teeth. In time, people learned how to carve stone into ornaments.

The ancient world
People discovered how to work with metals. Gold became highly valued, partly because it is easily worked and does not tarnish. Some of the finest surviving examples of gold jewellery were crafted more than 4,500 years ago, by the Sumerians. Amulets had been important since prehistoric times, and the ancient Egyptians often incorporated them into rings and other jewellery. In ancient Greece and Rome, the best-quality jewellery was

made from gold and silver and decorated with gemstones. Cheap jewellery was made from bronze, iron and even lead. Independent designs and techniques were developed by central and northwestern European peoples, such as the Celts.

The Middle Ages
Earrings and bracelets were rarely worn in Europe by the late Middle Ages, although brooches and necklaces remained popular. From the 13th century onwards, laws were passed preventing ordinary people from owning precious jewellery. Purses were hung from a beltlike girdle, and gloves were widely worn. Sophisticated gem-cutting techniques were imported from Persia and India in the 14th century.

16th century
Sumptuous jewellery and jewel-encrusted garments were worn at the European royal courts. Although brooches had fallen from favour, earrings had become fashionable again by the century's end and were worn by stylish noblemen and women. Noblewomen also began attaching jewels and gold ornaments to their hair.

17th century
Folding fans and gauntlet-style gloves had become key accessories, and wealthy women began carrying parasols. Brooches came back into fashion, and flowers and bows were popular motifs for all forms of jewellery. Men began tying small scarves, called cravats, around their necks.

18th century
Bracelets became popular again, and sets of jewellery called parures were worn by women. The French Revolution (1789–99) swept away the extravagance of the French nobility, and Europe became gripped by a passion for simplicity. Men stopped wearing most jewellery, apart from rings. Stylish women began wearing skimpy gowns that offered little protection in cold weather and no room for a pocket. Stoles and handbags, called reticules, became fashionable. A few men began carrying umbrellas.

19th century
Women's handbag styles multiplied and men began wearing neckties. The choker was a popular necklace style, and wealthy women wore tiaras on special occasions. New machinery made the mass production of cheap jewellery possible, and clip and screw fastenings were introduced for earrings.

20th century & beyond
By the 1920s, watches were being worn by both sexes, while costume jewellery took off in the 1930s. Mass production continued to make stylish jewellery widely available, but the 20th century also saw the rise in popularity of handmade pieces by artist jewellers. From the 1960s onwards, it became fashionable once more for men to wear jewellery. Since the 1990s, electronic accessories such as the mobile phone have become ever more essential.

Glossary

Amulet

A charm which the wearer believes has magic powers to protect against evil or disease. Amulets have been around since prehistoric times, and were often worn on necklaces.

Bakelite

An early type of plastic, invented by American chemist Leo Hendrik Baekeland (1863–1944) and patented in 1909.

Carat

A unit equal to 0.2 grams, which is used for weighing precious stones. In ancient times, plant seeds were used as weights, and the word comes from the Arabic for a seed or bean. The term carat is also used as a measure for the purity of gold, with the purest gold being 24 carats.

Circlet

A simple, hoop-shaped head ornament.

Costume jewellery

A 20th-century term for jewellery made from inexpensive or synthetic materials. It is not a modern invention, however. People have been making fake pearls since medieval times, for instance.

Gemstone

A precious or semi-precious stone, especially one that has been cut and polished for setting into jewellery. Precious gems include diamond, emerald, ruby and sapphire. Semi-precious gems include amethyst, opal and topaz. Nearly all are minerals. The four non-mineral gemstones are amber, coral, jet and pearls.

Lapidary

The craft of cutting and polishing gemstones, which dates back more than 6,000 years.

Parure

A co-ordinating set of jewellery, such as a necklace, earrings and bracelet all made with matching materials and design.

Pendant

An ornament designed to hang from a necklace or other piece of jewellery.

Tiara

An ornamental headdress which rises to a peak above the forehead. Unlike a crown, a tiara is backless and does not encircle the entire head.

Wreath

A garland usually made of real flowers or plant leaves. In the past, however, wreaths for the head were sometimes made from precious metals, with the flowers or leaves crafted in gold or silver.

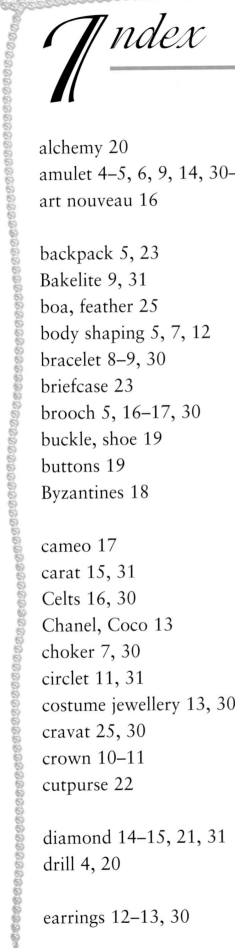

Index